mission shaped intro

What is a fresh expression of church?

A **fresh expression** is a form of church for our changing culture, established primarily for the benefit of people who are not yet members of any church.

It will come into being through principles of listening, service, incarnational mission and making disciples.

It will have the potential to become a mature expression of church shaped by the gospel and the enduring marks of the church and for its cultural context.

Fresh expressions of church:

- serve those outside church;
- listen to people and enter their culture;
- make discipleship a priority;
- form church.

Fresh Expressions exists to encourage and resource these new ways of being church, working with Christians from a broad range of denominations and traditions. The movement has resulted in thousands of new congregations being formed alongside more traditional churches.

Contents

Introduction

The overall aim of *mission shaped intro* is to give people a fresh vision of mission and how we might reshape the church in the light of our ever-changing modern culture.

About the course

mission shaped intro is designed to inform you about the changing culture of today's society and the responses needed to engage in mission in meaningful and relevant ways. It won't equip you to go out and start fresh expressions, but it will challenge your thinking.

If you are looking for a course which explores how to start and sustain a fresh expression of church, visit the website to find out about the *mission shaped ministry* course, a one-year, part-time course which trains participants for ministry in fresh expressions of church.

Course website, for updates to the notes, additional materials, course fliers, registration and feedback and other information.
bit.ly/msicourse

mission shaped intro web page
freshexpressions.org.uk/missionshapedintro

mission shaped ministry web page
freshexpressions.org.uk/missionshapedministry

One of the most important resources for those in fresh expressions of church is the Guide, an online learning resource. Pages helpful for this session are highlighted throughout these notes.
freshexpressions.org.uk/guide

⟋ Aim

 Recommended reading

Core resources for the course

Recommended reading

Books

- **Mission-shaped Church (second edition)**
  Graham Cray, CHP, 2004, 978-071514189-2.

- **Fresh! An introduction to fresh expressions of church and pioneer ministry**
  David Goodhew, Andrew Roberts, Michael Volland, SCM, 2012, 978-033404387-4.

- **Church for every context: An introduction to theology and practice**
  Michael Moynagh, SCM Press, 2012, 978-033404369-0

- **changing church for a changing world**
  Pete Pillinger, Andrew Roberts, MPH, 2007, 978-185852335-4.

- **Pioneers 4 Life ***
  David Male (ed.), BRF, 2011, 978-184101827-0.

- **Resourcing Renewal: Shaping Churches for the Emerging Future ***
  Martyn Atkins, Inspire, 2007, 978-190595810-8.

- **God-Shaped Mission: Theological and Practical Perspectives from the Rural Church ***
  Alan Smith, Canterbury Press Norwich, 2008, 978-185311807-4.

DVDs

- **expressions: making a difference**
  Norman Ivison, Fresh Expressions, 2011, 978-0-9560005-4-5.

- **Sanctus: fresh expressions of church in the sacramental tradition**
  Norman Ivison, Fresh Expressions, 2009, 978-0-9560005-3-8.

- **expressions: the dvd - 2: changing church in every place**
  Norman Ivison, CHP, 2007, 978-071514128-1.

- **expressions: the dvd - 1: stories of church for a changing culture**
  Norman Ivison, CHP, 2006, 978-071514095-6.

Fresh Expressions
freshexpressions.org.uk

The Guide, exploring fresh expressions of church together
freshexpressions.org.uk/guide

Fresh Expressions online shop, where you can purchase all resources on this page except those marked *
freshexpressions.org.uk/shop

Share booklets

- **How can fresh expressions emerge? (Share booklet 01)**
  Michael Moynagh with Andy Freeman, Fresh Expressions, 2011, 978-0-9568123-1-5.

- **How should we start? (Share booklet 02)**
  Michael Moynagh with…, Fresh Expressions, 2011, 978-0-9568123-2-2.

- **What should we start? (Share booklet 03)**
  Michael Moynagh with…, Fresh Expressions, 2011, 978-0-9568123-3-9.

- **How can we get support? (Share booklet 04)**
  Michael Moynagh with…, Fresh Expressions, 2011, 978-0-9568123-4-6.

- **How can we find our way? (Share booklet 05)**
  Michael Moynagh with…, Fresh Expressions, 2011, 978-0-9568123-5-3.

- **How can we be sustainable? (Share booklet 06)**
  Michael Moynagh with…, Fresh Expressions, 2011, 978-0-9568123-6-0.

- **How can we be a great team? (Share booklet 07)**
  Michael Moynagh with…, Fresh Expressions, 2011, 978-0-9568123-7-7.

- **How can we finance a fresh expression? (Share booklet 08)**
  John Preston, Andrew Roberts, Fresh Expressions, 2012, 978-095681238-4.

- **How can we encourage a fresh expression? (Share booklet 09)**
  Michael Moynagh, Fresh Expressions, 2012, 978-095681239-1.

- **How should we teach and preach? (Share booklet 10)**
  Norman Ivison, Fresh Expressions, 2013, 978-095756840-2.

Further titles are released regularly, visit the Share booklets page at freshexpressions.org.uk/share/booklets for the latest information.

1. rediscovering mission - what that means for the church

Section one: welcome, introductions and worship

 Aim

To explore the mission of God as the foundation for any expression of church test.

Rediscovering mission - what that means for the church

Section one: welcome, introductions and worship

Welcome and group introductions

Worship and prayer

Section two: introducing Mission-shaped Church

About the report

Section three: stories of fresh expressions

Stories of fresh expressions

Your response - small group discussion and plenary discussion

Section four: our changing world

Film clip

Changes in society

Section five: worship

Pause for praise

Section six: what would a mission-shaped church look like?

Mission is..., marks of mission

Your church mission-shaped

Closing prayer and worship

Jeff Reynolds' Story

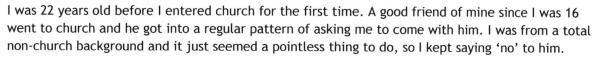

I was 22 years old before I entered church for the first time. A good friend of mine since I was 16 went to church and he got into a regular pattern of asking me to come with him. I was from a total non-church background and it just seemed a pointless thing to do, so I kept saying 'no' to him.

Eventually I made a pact with him that if I went to church just once, he would promise never to ask me again. That would enable me to stop finding creative ways of saying 'no' to a good friend. The great day came and the service began at 6.30pm. I said to my friend that I would get there at 6.29 and sneak in at the back. My first major error was to then completely forget the starting time. Come the said day I had convinced myself that I needed to be there at 5.59 for a 6pm start. This I duly did and found myself wandering into a nearly empty church.

Now I need to say that I'm 6ft 2in tall and it was summer time so I was in my t-shirt, shaven-headed with the swagger of a young twenty-something who did a bit of boxing. There was a lady sitting on the back row, she took one look at me and immediately picked up her handbag and held it tightly. Obviously, I looked an undesirable and some kind of potential thief - welcome to Church! The person on the door had given me two hymn books, a Bible, notice sheet and song sheet because apparently one song wasn't in any of the books and we would be singing it in the service. Very bewildering for a totally non-churched person.

The Church filled up and the service began with a man appearing at the front from a hole in the wall. He was obviously in a rush as he had his shirt on back to front! We then sang a series of songs I didn't know and which were basically impossible to sing with archaic lyrics and bizarre tunes. We sat down and the man at the front led us in prayer. It was at this point that I nearly put my hand up and asked him what prayer was, because I didn't know, but everybody else seemed to know and they all crouched forward like they were preparing for a scrummage but they had their eyes shut.

Next we had a reading from the book of Obadiah. By the time I'd found it (with the help of the index) it had finished. The man at the front, who was by now sweating profusely, spoke at us for about 20 minutes. It was utter drivel with very forced humour and I realised that it was 20 minutes of my life that I would never get back. To cap it all, they had the sheer cheek to ask for money for this 'worship experience!' I was tempted to take a fiver out rather than put 10p in as the plate passed by. I couldn't get out fast enough and won't tell you my response to my friend who said to me after the service, 'did you enjoy that?' Perhaps the most bizarre and baffling part of this story is that I went back the next week and am now the Superintendent of the Stafford Methodist Circuit.

Section two: introducing *Mission-shaped Church*

About the report

Despite all the press reports of falling numbers, there are encouraging signs that a springtime season is beginning in the life of the church, with new growth springing up everywhere.

A fresh expression is a form of church for our changing culture established primarily for the benefit of people who are not yet members of any church.

We need to learn to be a both/and church:

* **both** treasuring what we have inherited in the church
* **and** valuing and developing the newer forms

Section three: stories of fresh expressions

Stories of fresh expressions

Your responses and reactions.

Section four: our changing world

Changes in society

We need to respond to the fact that society is always changing, with the pace of change increasing in recent years. In twos or threes, list some of the changes in society that have an impact on the way that we do church, or the assumptions we make about church.

Theology - missiology - ecclesiology

Our theology affects our missiology which determines our ecclesiology.

Or in English:

- our understanding of God the Father, Son and Holy Spirit,
- must unpack itself through our understanding of mission,
- which then shapes the church,

not the other way round.

A fresh expression is a form of church for our changing culture established primarily for the benefit of people who are not yet members of any church.

It will come into being through principles of listening, service, incarnational mission and making disciples.

It will have the potential to become a mature expression of church, shaped by the Gospel and the enduring historic marks of the church within and for its cultural context.

Section six: what would a mission-shaped church look like?

 What Christian principles lie behind fresh expressions?
freshexpressions.org.uk/guide/about/principles

Mission is...

Mission is seeing what God is doing and joining in.

In groups of three or four, create the three priorities you think God wants the church (us) to engage with.

Marks of mission

The word mission has Latin roots - misseo - meaning 'to be sent'.

God shines his light through the prism of mission producing these colours:

Red	A 'loud' colour, heralding	Proclaim the Good News of the Kingdom.
Orange Yellow	Colours of spring, new life, new start	To teach, baptize and nurture new believers.
Green	Pastoral, earth, association of the colour with environmental responsibility	To strive to safeguard the integrity of creation and sustain and renew the life of the earth.
Blue	Colour of peace, wholeness and healing	To respond to human need by loving service.
Indigo Violet	Purple, colours of authority, sovereignty, power	To seek to transform unjust structures of society.

2. changing world, changing church

Section one: welcome, introductions and worship

 Aim

To explore how the church might respond to a world of change and uncertainty.

Section two: the church's response to uncertainty

Exploring uncertainty

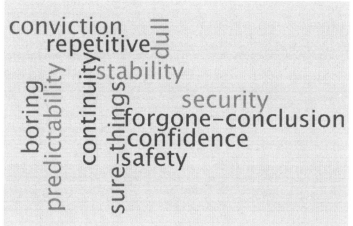

conviction
repetitive
dull
stability
continuity
boring
predictability
sure-things
security
forgone–conclusion
confidence
safety

What does certainty feel like? What are the keywords for certainty?

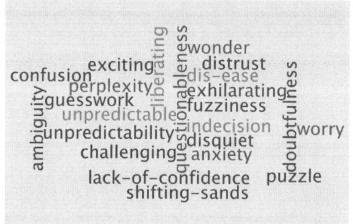

liberating
wonder
exciting
distrust
confusion
dis-ease
perplexity
questionableness
exhilarating
doubtfulness
guesswork
fuzziness
unpredictable
ambiguity
unpredictability
indecision
worry
disquiet
challenging
anxiety
lack-of-confidence
puzzle
shifting–sands

What does uncertainty feel like? What are the keywords for uncertainty?

Group exercise

This exercise aims to explore a loss of certainty of the past ten years. In your groups, please come up with examples of things that have happened over the past decade which have made people less certain about their lives in an unhelpful way.

Our response to uncertainty

Uncertainty is clearly a negative thing when it:

*   makes us take dangerous risks;
*   leads to a lack of emotional security.

Uncertainty can be a good thing when it:

*   challenges us to think and work hard;
*   develops our 'creative' muscles;
*   awakens us;
*   allows mystery and wonder;
*   leads us to recognise our need of God.

A faithful Church is continually shaped by its inner dynamic: the flow of Apostolic Tradition, with Scripture as its norm... The Church is, however, also shaped by the kind of world in which it finds itself. This must mean a constant receiving of the Gospel into our particular context.
Michael Nazir-Ali, Future Shapes of the Church *(House of Bishops paper, 2001) quoted in Mission-shaped Church, p91*

How do people respond to uncertainty? They may:

- panic;
- feel lost or disoriented;
- dig in stubbornly;
- spend!;
- opt out.

We respond to uncertainty in positive ways by considering:

- what we build;
- how we plan;
- how we think.

Some key questions to ponder are:

1. Can we plan well when we can't be sure of anything?
2. What are the better ways to approach mission initiatives and develop fresh expressions of church in uncertain times?
3. People do need fixed points of reference, points of security, familiarity - what are these and how are they expressed in church and Christian community?
4. Could the value of church seasons and rhythms of life be helpfully rediscovered in these uncertain times?

A story

Discuss how the fresh expression featured is building or planning in an uncertain world.

- answers are more convergent;
- questions are more divergent;
- answers tend to tell us 'what to think';
- questions tend to help us with 'how to think'.

Group exercise

In your groups, imagine you are meeting with a group of people exploring the Christian faith. In the news that week there has been a major event that has shaken people (it could have been a financial collapse or a natural disaster or some other unforeseen event). Conscious that people will be mindful of this event, prepare an outline for the meeting in which you will explore either John 14.5-6 or Hebrews 11.1-2. No 20-minute sermons allowed!

Section three: thinking about networks

Introduction to networks

In Britain denominational planning has depended too exclusively on the "geographical map". Within the Church of England this has been influenced by the parish structure from rural society with a feudal structure. While the geographical map may be helpful to ensure a measure of blanket coverage, it can at the same time be misleading if used as the only planning model.
Eddie Gibbs, I believe in Church Growth, *p95*

Now the eleven disciples went to Galilee, to the mountain to which Jesus had directed them. When they saw him, they worshipped him; but some doubted. And Jesus came and said to them, 'All authority in heaven and on earth has been given to me. Go therefore and make disciples of all nations, baptizing them in the name of the Father and of the Son and of the Holy Spirit, and teaching them to obey everything that I have commanded you. And remember, I am with you always, to the end of the age.'
Matthew 28.16-20

Identifying networks we belong to

Responding to networks

 Fresh expressions reach out to post-modern society
freshexpressions.org.uk/guide/about/why/postmodern

Section four: more about mission

Recommend resources

A new way of thinking about mission

Fresh expressions involve a new way of thinking about mission.

Church for my friend

Individually, think of a friend who is not part of a church community. Bearing in mind all that we have said, what would a church where your friend feels welcome and at home look and feel like? How might they get involved? When and where would it meet? What kind of opportunities for gathering might it provide? What might happen there?

That's not to say that each person can expect a church that is tailor-made for them, or that panders to their taste. But if we were to start with this person and with what God is doing in their life, what kind of church might we end up with?

When you have considered these questions, share your thoughts in twos, or if you are with a group from your church, that group.

Recommended resources

- **fresh! An introduction to fresh expressions of church and pioneer ministry**
  David Goodhew, Andrew Roberts, Michael Volland, SCM Press, 2012, 978-033404387-4

- **Church Unplugged: Remodelling Church Without Losing Your soul**
  David Male, Authentic, 2008, 978-185078792-1.

- **Changing World, Changing Church**
  Michael Moynagh, Monarch Books, 2001, 978-1854245168.

- **Church after Christendom**
  Stuart Murray, Paternoster, 2005, 978-184227292-3.

3. re-imagining church - community

Section one: welcome, introductions and worship

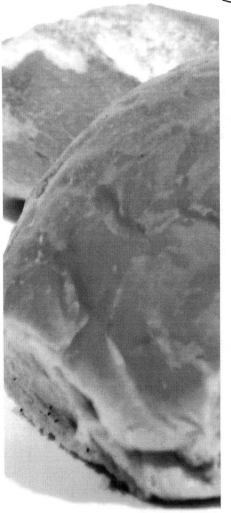

 Aim

To explore the need for fresh expressions of church to develop authentic community in a world shaped by consumerism and individualism.

Re-imagining church - community

Section one: welcome, introductions and worship

Introduction, recap sessions one and two

Worship and prayer

Section two: belonging

Belonging

Where do you belong?

Section three: consumerism, good or bad?

Me spirituality

Story

Section four: what kind of community?

Rewriting Acts 2

Pause for prayer

Community within the church

  How can we do this?

Open to the community around us

  How can we do this?

Section five: final worship

Worship and prayer

Section two: belonging

Belonging

1. Public space
2. Social space
3. Personal space
4. Intimate space

Where do you belong?

Section three: consumerism, good or bad?

Me spirituality

> *It's not about the money, money, money*
> *We don't need your money, money, money*
> *We just wanna make the world dance, forget about the price tag.*
> *Why is everybody so obsessed? Money can't buy us happiness*
> *Can we all slow down and enjoy right now, guarantee we'll be*
> *feelin' all right.*
> **Jessie J, Price Tag**

> *Worship is a form of entertainment... If people are not entertained,*
> *they don't feel that they are participating.*
> **Washington Post, 05/01/03**

Consumer culture does create opportunities for mission and service. Here are a few ways some churches are engaging with those who need serving:

1. Offering Christian Spirituality courses at the local college
2. Life coaching
3. Parenting Classes

Story

Section four: what kind of community?

Rewriting Acts 2

Read Acts 2.42-47 and in small groups re-write it in its opposite sense.

> *They devoted themselves to the apostles' teaching and fellowship, to the breaking of bread and the prayers. Awe came upon everyone, because many wonders and signs were being done by the apostles. All who believed were together and had all things in common; they would sell their possessions and goods and distribute the proceeds to all, as any had need. Day by day, as they spent much time together in the temple, they broke bread at home and ate their food with glad and generous hearts, praising God and having the goodwill of all the people. And day by day the Lord added to their number those who were being saved.*
> **Acts 2.42-47**

> *The portrayal may be somewhat idealized... But anyone who is familiar with movements of enthusiastic spiritual renewal will recognise authentic notes: the enthusiasm of the members of the renewal group, with a sense of overflowing joy (Acts 2.46), desire to come together frequently (Acts 2.44,46), eating together and worshipping (Acts 2.46-47) and including the readiness for unreserved commitment to one another in a shared common life.*
> **James Dunn, The Acts of the Apostles, Epworth, 1996, p34**

When asked how other could start a fresh expression, teenager Ruth at The Bridge in Hinckley said 'talk together, eat together, pray together'. Very good advice!

Community within the church

The early church was:

- not over-organised.
- not too centralised.
- simply God's people getting on with being Christians in society.
- liked by the wider community!

The only hermeneutic of the Gospel is a congregation of men and women who believe it and live by it. The church is to be the primary agent of mission and if it does not exhibit evident community and transformed lives then any amount of evangelistic events and church projects will have limited credibility.
Lesslie Newbigin, The Gospel in a Pluralist society, SPCK, 2004, p227

Genuine community requires:

- honesty;
- effort;
- reality;
- peace.

From whom the whole body, joined and knitted together by every ligament with which it is equipped, as each part is working properly, promotes the body's growth in building itself up in love.
Ephesians 4.16

Definition

hermeneutic
interpretation, explanation, making clear, understanding of.

How can we do this?

Here are some biblical verse that provide guidance for deep and meaningful relationships.

Love one another with mutual affection; outdo one another in showing honour - Romans 12.10

Be kind to one another, tender-hearted, forgiving one another as God in Christ has forgiven you - Ephesians 4.32

But exhort one another every day - Hebrews 3.13

Provoke one another to love and good deeds - Hebrews 10.24

Therefore confess your sins to one another, and pray for one another, so that you may be healed - James 5.16

Bear one another's burdens - Galatians 6.2

Welcome one another - Romans 15.7

Be subject to one another out of reverence for Christ - Ephesians 5.21

But through love become slaves to one another - Galatians 5.13

Bear with one another - Colossians 3.13

Adapted from Phil Potter, The Challenge of Cell Church, BRF, 2001.

Open to the community around us

We need total attentive listening involving:

- listening to God;
- listening to each other;
- listening to those beyond the church.

Jesus presents us with a dream (embodied in the group image 'Kingdom of God') that is irreducibly communal, familial and social. It is not just a dream of more and better individual Christians standing like isolated statues in a museum. It is a dream of a community vibrant with life, pulsating with forgiveness, loud with celebration, fruitful in mission... a substantial city whose streets bustle with life, whose buildings echo with praise, a city aglow with the glory of community.
Brian D. McLaren, The Church on the Other Side: Doing Ministry in the Postmodern Matrix, Zondervan, 2002, 978-031025219-1

How can we do this?

- What has been the most striking thing you have heard about community tonight?
- Is there one thing you might do to help build community?

Recommended resources

Recommended resources

- **Cave Refectory Road: Monastic Rhythms for contemporary living**
  Ian Adams, Canterbury Press Norwich, 2010,
  978-184825028-4.

- **The Hospitality of God**
  Mary Gray-Reeves & Michael Perham, SPCK, 2011,
  978-028106350-5.

- **The Search to belong: Rethinking intimacy, community and small groups**
  Joseph R. Myers, Zondervan, 2003, 978-031025500-0.

- **Through the Pilgrim Door**
  Michael Volland, DC Cook, 2009, 978-184291399-4.

 God works through communities
freshexpressions.org.uk/guide/about/principles/communities

The IN dimension of church
freshexpressions.org.uk/guide/about/proper/in

web

4. re-imagining church - worship

Section one: welcome, introductions and worship

 Aim

To explore how fresh expressions of church are re-imagining worship.

Section two: what is worship?

Draw a chair

What is worship?

The church must be like water - flexible, fluid, changeable.
Pete Ward

Section three: re-imagining worship

Creative worship

Creative worship...

• reframes tradition;

> *[The greatest gift fresh expressions can offer to the whole church is a] sense of confidence in what we have been given and its potential to draw us and others more effectively into the experience of the love and beauty and holiness of God. Such confidence will make us more creative and more adventurous in our worship and will allow the grace of God to be experienced both in the traditional things we shall do better and in the new things we shall do well.*
> **Michael Perham, Mary Gray-Reeves, The Hospitality of God, SPCK, 2011, p146**

• uses contemporary culture;

• is multi-sensory;

• is participative;

• is accessible to all;

• creates space for a response (but not a uniform one).

Section four: experiencing creative worship

Worship stations

Section five: making changes

How can we re-imagine worship?

Day by day, as they spent much time together in the temple, they broke bread at home and ate their food with glad and generous hearts, praising God and having the goodwill of all the people. And day by day the Lord added to their number those who were being saved.
Acts 2.46-47

* start small, start at the edges
* create worship from the gifts and resources that you have
* connect with other groups to see what they do
* embrace your creativity!

Creating worship

Your task is to come up with a creative worship or prayer idea that combines the three elements that you have been given. It may feel a little contrived to be given these parameters, but the reality of creativity is that we often respond well to these kinds of restrictions, rather than starting with a completely blank sheet of paper. You have ten minutes to come up with your idea and then we're going to hear from each group.

Recommended resources

Recommended resources

 50 Worship Ideas for Small Groups
Stuart Townend, Morgan Lewis, Kingsway, 2000, 978-184291279-9.

Curating Worship
Jonny Baker, SPCK, 2010, 978-028106235-5.

Emerging Churches: Creating Christian Communities in Postmodern Cultures
Eddie Gibbs, Ryan K Bolger, SPCK, 2006, 978-028105791-7.

Messy Church series
Lucy Moore, see messychurch.org.uk/pages/3520.htm for details.

Creative Ideas for Alternative Sacramental Worship
Simon Rundell, Canterbury Press, 2010, 978-184825023-9.

 The UP dimension of church
freshexpressions.org.uk/guide/about/proper/up

5. re-imagining church - discipleship and leadership

Section one: welcome, introductions and worship

 Aim

To explore how to enable healthy discipleship and leadership within fresh expressions of church.

Section two: valuing creativity

Made in the image of God

The modern world was grounded. Its favorite definition of God was 'Ground of Being'. Its basic metaphors were drawn from a landscape consciousness that didn't trust water. Scholars are trained to keep categories clean and 'watertight'. We were taught to avoid watering down our insights. The surface on which we lived was solid, fixed, and predictable. We could get the lay of the land, mark off directions where we were headed, and follow maps and blueprints to get where we were going. Much time, energy, and even spilt blood were devoted to defending, maintaining, and marking off our boundaries. Border disputes were common and devastating.

Postmodern culture has marched off all maps. Its environment is a seascape; its surface is fluid and not fixed. It changes with every gust of wind and every wave. It is always unpredictable. Old maps and blueprints are useless on an uncharted, ever changing seascape. The sea knows no boundaries. The only way to get where one is going on a seascape is through nautical skill and trajectories rather than through fixed and clearly identified roads and highways. In this world, fluidity wins over fixity. Instead of structuring and ordering and solidifying reality, cyberspace bends and melts it. Life is a fluid realm. Fluid however, does not mean anything goes, as any capable ship captain will quickly affirm. Fluid is a different kind of order, a different kind of going.
Leonard Sweet, Soul Tsunami: Sink or Swim in New Millennium Culture, Zondervan, 1999

Church culture:

- can stifle creativity
- or it can foster creativity

Section three: discipleship

Thinking about discipleship

> *Now the eleven disciples went to Galilee, to the mountain to which Jesus had directed them. When they saw him, they worshipped him; but some doubted. And Jesus came and said to them, 'All authority in heaven and on earth has been given to me. Go therefore and make disciples of all nations, baptizing them in the name of the Father and of the Son and of the Holy Spirit, and teaching them to obey everything that I have commanded you. And remember, I am with you always, to the end of the age.'*
> *Matthew 28.16-20*

1. discipleship - a journey, not a crisis event

2. believe; behave; belong and bless?

3. what sort of journey?
   - a lifelong apprenticeship;
   - lived out in the whole of life, not just the 'churchy' bits;
   - an adventure;
   - communal;
   - biblical;
   - cross-shaped;
   - sacramental;
   - reproducing;
   - a model of the kingdom;
   - a growing thing;
   - the key to resourcing new forms of church;
   - the spiritual soil in which Christian leaders grow.

How was it for you?

- How did the journey begin for you?
- What has helped you to grow as a disciple of Jesus?

Developing discipleship in fresh expressions

1. Supportive relationships

- companions are those who walk alongside each other as equals.
- mentors and apprentices.

Small groups provide safe environments for individuals:

- to ask questions;
- to discuss aspects of the faith;
- to get to know a limited number of people well and develop a sense of belonging;
- to provide prayer and pastoral support for each other;
- to learn how to share their gifts and minister to one another.

2. Teaching and learning

When developing materials 'in house' it is important to ask critical questions such as

- is it biblical?
- is it true to the Christian tradition?
- is it whole-life?
- is it both open and challenging?

Some ideas

- include an explicitly Christian dimension from an early stage.
- include a more general spiritual dimension from an early stage.
- create opportunities to form a separate discipleship group.

Group work

Think how you would prepare a group of people new to the Christian faith for the journey of discipleship? Consider:

- Who would be part of the journey? Don't forget Jesus! Note how those exploring faith can sharpen faith in others - healthy discipleship communities are places of mutual learning, not groups of experts and empty vessels. Jesus used the questions and comments of others to allow truth to emerge in the midst of conversation.
- What resources or tools would take to guide and equip you?
- What food would sustain you on the journey?
- How would you travel? What rhythms might you follow, where and when might you meet to communicate, what significant markers might you look for on the journey?
- What would you do?

Leadership in a fresh expression of church

1. Christian discipleship is foundational for Christian leadership.
2. Leaders come in all shapes and sizes and all Christians have their part to play in Christian leadership.
3. Christian leadership is not confined to the Church!

Leadership is about:

*   noticing and discerning potential and putting your own reputation on the line when appropriate (Acts 9.23-30);
*   spending time mentoring other people (Acts 11.25-30);
*   being chosen, commissioned and prayerfully set aside for a task by a bigger group of people (Acts 12.25-13.3);
*   stepping up at the opportune moment and letting the succession continue (Acts 13.4-12);
*   using your experience and background as well as knowing the context to which you are speaking (Acts 13.16-45);
*   accepting persecution (Acts 13.46-52);
*   knowing when to leave and when to stay (Acts 14.1-7);
*   pointing to someone greater (Acts 14.8-18);
*   being ready to get hurt (Acts 14.19-20);
*   being accountable and testifying honestly to what God is doing (Acts 14.26-28);
*   asking tough theological questions and wrestling with the answers in the midst of those wiser and more discerning (Acts 15.1-21);
*   discerning the right team at the right time (Acts 15.22-35);
*   being ready for conflict - succession is a mark of success (Acts 15.36-41).

Further qualities that leaders of fresh expressions of church will need:

- willingness to take risks;
- leading together;
- able to learn and adapt;

Exercise

What sort of leaders would you need for your chosen scenario? Describe their roles and the gifts and character you would be looking for:

1. You are a team planting a fresh expression of church in one of the following:

    - a residential home for elderly people;
    - an academy or high school;
    - a village hall;
    - a Messy Church;
    - a scenario of your own choice appropriate to your own context.

2. You are a church excited by what you have learnt on *msi* and are looking to become more mission-shaped.

Recommended resources

- **Disciples and Citizens: A Vision for Distinctive Living**
  Graham Cray, IVP, 2007, 978-1844741517-1.

- **Finding Our Way Again: The Return of the Ancient Practices**
  Brian McLaren, Thomas Nelson Publishers, 2008, 978-084994602-8.

- **The Call and the Commission: Equipping a New Generation of Leaders for a New World**
  Rob Frost, David Wilkinson and Joanne Cox (eds.), Paternoster, 2009, 978-1842276082.

- **Growing Leaders: Reflections on Leadership, Life and Jesus**
  James Lawrence, BRF, 2004, 978-1841012469.

- deepeningdiscipleship.org.uk.

 God grows church through reproduction
freshexpressions.org.uk/guide/about/principles/reproduction

God wants people to become disciples of Jesus
freshexpressions.org.uk/guide/about/principles/disciples

6. where do we go from here?

Section one: welcome, introductions and worship

 ## Aim

To provide space for people to consider their response to this course and what they might do next.

Section two: from listening to action

Listening - a key skill

In this session we're looking at what happens next. So far we have shown:

- how the mission belongs to God and is shaped by God's character;
- that it is God who invites us to join in;
- that the church is the fruit of mission and not vice versa;
- how these are exciting times in the life of the church;
- that for the new to emerge, sometimes we have to stop things.

As we think about developing fresh expressions of church, there are three vital strands that need to develop alongside each other.

1. prayer and support;
2. connection;
3. listening to God.

Daring to dream

Dare to dream! Don't let the sceptics and naysayers hold sway. For the next 25 minutes the following phrases are banned:

- it will never work;
- we couldn't do that;
- we've tried that before.

Section three: my response

What journey have you been on?

Next steps

Thank you from Fresh Expressions!

On behalf of Fresh Expressions, thank you for participating in *mission shaped intro*. You have joined people around the UK and on every continent who have used *msi* to help shape their thinking about the forms of church needed to partner in God's mission. We hope you find the following ways to continue your mission-shaped journey helpful.

Andrew Roberts, Director of Training, Fresh Expressions

Sharing what you have learned

To share what you have learned you could:

- host a *vision day* in your area: freshexpressions.org.uk/vision.
- purchase and share one of our DVDs which are full of stories of a wide range of fresh expressions: freshexpressions.org.uk/shop/listing/dvds. Our latest DVD is freshexpressions.org.uk/resources/makingadifference.
- use our *mission shaped congregations* CD-ROM which has lots of material for a service or small group thinking about fresh expressions of church: freshexpressions.org.uk/resources/congregations.

To keep in touch with Fresh Expressions you could:

- visit our website at freshexpressions.org.uk.
- sign up for our free monthly e-newsletter at freshexpressions.org.uk/signup.
- follow us on facebook.com/freshexpression, twitter.com/freshexpression or youtube.com/freshexpressions.

Going deeper

To go deeper in your thinking you could:

- read *Fresh! An introduction to fresh expressions of church and pioneer ministry*, offering practical guidance and best practice for starting and sustaining a fresh expression of church: freshexpressions.org.uk/resources/fresh.

- purchase *Church for every context*, an in depth exploration of the theology and methodology of fresh expressions of church: freshexpressions.org.uk/resources/context.

- read the *Share booklets* series which explore how to start and sustain fresh expressions of church - how should we start, how can we get support, how can we be a great team, how can we encourage a fresh expression and more: freshexpressions.org.uk/share/booklets.

- Join a *mission shaped ministry* course, the natural follow-on to *msi*, which explores in depth and detail the values, strategies and practices that lie behind fruitful mission-shaped churches freshexpressions.org.uk/missionshapedministry.

Supporting fresh expressions

To support the ongoing work of Fresh Expressions financially you could:

- give online, by phone or by post: freshexpressions.org.uk/support.

- give by text by texting 'FRES12 £10' (or £5, £4, £3, £2 or £1) to 70070.

Texts are charged at your mobile phone operator's standard rate. The charity will receive 100% of your donation. You must be 16 or over and please ask the bill payer's permission. For full terms and conditions and more information, please visit justgiving.com/info/terms-of-service.

Published 2013 by Fresh Expressions
Registered charity #1080103

Copyright © Fresh Expressions 2013
freshexpressions.org.uk

Fresh Expressions, The Benn Centre,
Claremont Road, Rugby, CV21 3LU
0300 365 0563

Author: Fresh Expressions
Contributors: See full credits to the right
Designer: Ben Clymo

freshexpressions.org.uk/
missionshapedintro

ISBN 978-0-9560005-6-9

fresh expressions

Credits

This course was first devised and run by Tony Hardy of CPAS and Sally Thornton.

Further revisions and editing by Ian Adams, Tim Atkins, Jenny Baker, Kelly Betteridge, Karen Carter, Ben Clymo, Ross Garner, Bev Hollings, Norman Ivison, Rachel Jordan, Phil Joyce, Tim Lea, Bruce and Colleen Mounsey, Sheonagh Ormrod, Ruth Poch, Jeff Reynolds, Andrew Roberts, Pam Smith, Martyn Snow, Sally Thornton and Tim Woolley.

Partners

Thanks to our *msi* partners: Church Army, Church of England, CMS, Congregational Federation, CWM Europe, Ground Level Network, Methodist Church, United Reformed Church.

Course workbook

The course notes and DVD for teachers (978-09560005-5-2) are available to purchase from our online shop: freshexpressions.org.uk/shop.